Coaching

Coaching Strategies

The Top 100 Best Ways To Be A Great Coach

By Ace McCloud
Copyright © 2016

Disclaimer

The information provided in this book is designed to provide helpful information on the subjects discussed. This book is not meant to be used, nor should it be used, to diagnose or treat any medical condition. For diagnosis or treatment of any medical problem, consult your own physician. The publisher and author are not responsible for any specific health or allergy needs that may require medical supervision and are not liable for any damages or negative consequences from any treatment, action, application or preparation, to any person reading or following the information in this book. Any references included are provided for informational purposes only. Readers should be aware that any websites or links listed in this book may change.

Table of Contents

Introduction 6
Chapter 1: Leadership and Coaching 7
Chapter 2: Form a Winning Team 14
Chapter 3: Prepare Them Physically................... 24
Chapter 4: Prepare Them Mentally To Compete ... 40
Chapter 5: Prepare to Win......................................54
Conclusion 61
My Other Books and Audio Books 62

Be sure to check out my website for all my Books and Audio books.

www.AcesEbooks.com

Introduction

I want to thank you and congratulate you for buying the book, "Coaching: Coaching Strategies: The Top 100 Best Ways to Be a Great Coach."

Coaching is the solid foundation behind any successful sports team. By definition, coaching is a training and development process that involves a supporter (the coach) and a learner (the player). The supporter often has years of expertise and experience beyond the learner, hence his ability to teach and pass on information. Unlike mentoring, coaching focuses more on teaching specific tasks and reaching specific goals. There are different types of coaching for different areas of life: General life coaching, health and wellness coaching, mental health coaching, business and career coaching, financial coaching, relationship coaching, and sports coaching. This book will focus on coaching for sports, although most of the strategies used are transferable to other areas of life.

The job of a sports coach is to help an athlete develop to his or her full potential. A coach will analyze a player's performance, instruct and advise in skills development and provide encouragement, among other things. To be a sports coach, you have to be not only a coach but also a leader, mentor, motivator and teacher.

Some great coaches have shown just how far powerful a coach's influence can take individual players as well as whole teams. In the chapters that follow we will briefly review the legacy of well-known individuals like Joe Paterno, Bobby Knight, Bill Walsh, Vince Lombardi, Red Auerbach, Phil Jackson, Eddie Robinson, and John Wooden. Each of these coaches has moved mountains in his particular sport, setting high standards for all who follow in his footsteps.

This book contains proven steps and strategies on how to become a powerful, successful and possibly legendary coach yourself. You will discover everything you need to know to help your team become unstoppable – including how to help athletes prepare physically and mentally, how to improve communication with your team, how to boost player morale, how to assist your players in developing new skills, and much more. It takes a very special and dedicated person to be a great coach – will it be you?

Chapter 1: Leadership and Coaching

Coaches are leaders whose every decision is put on display. A leader is a person with a clear vision for the future who wants to enlist others to help him turn a dream into reality. In the same way, a sports coach is pursuing an objective; he wants to build a team of players that will grow into both a successful performing unit and individual players who are learning and growing, both as athletes and as people.

A Coach:

- Analyzes individuals and teams, seeking insight as to how they work and how to optimize their performance.

- Coordinates multiple teams: teams of athletes, teams of staff, and teams of supporters.

- Mentors individuals, helping them overcome any obstacles that would hold them back from succeeding.

- Assists individuals as they develop into leaders in their own right.

- Equips individual leaders to pursue success in their field.

- Steers teams of leaders as they pursue their dreams.

- Inspires whole communities to reach for a vision.

Practical Dreamers

Leaders tend to view a person or a situation through two separate lenses. On the one hand, they are experts at grasping a non-sugar-coated understanding of the current reality. On the other, they are able to see beyond the present reality, stretching their vision to the extent that a person or a situation can be developed.

They are dreamers but also strategizers. They have both feet firmly planted in the present, but can cast a vision far into the future. They can successfully see ways around the obstacles in their path until the desired result is reached.

Due to their tendency to be internal visionaries, leaders may appear as somewhat aloof from reality. However, the air of confidence they draw from embracing a specific vision can infect their followers. A leader's certainty is powerful and can become a rallying point once the vision is communicated.

A coach needs to be able to capitalize on his knowledge of the needs, motivations, playing styles, and values of each member on the team. As a coach, you will use your knowledge of these people to meld them into a cohesive unit.

Essential Habits For Any Leader

Since leadership is an important foundation for any coach, it is your job to become the best leader possible. There are several key characteristics that are common among leaders. Building these habits into your life will improve your ability to lead.

1. **Be Optimistic** – People want to be around others who view life as a positive venture. As a coach, it is essential to be able to focus on the strengths of the people you are working with. While you are clear-sighted about difficulties, problems, and weaknesses, you view these not as impossible show-stoppers but as opportunities for you and others to grow and learn. The people in your life will love you for this.

2. **Be Committed** – When your players can see that you are committed to their individual success and the success of the team, not only will they respect you, but your commitment will motivate them to commit to both themselves and the team. Commitment is contagious; the more your team members sense that you're "all in," the more they will be, too.

3. **Model Integrity** – Not only is integrity good for your soul, research actually shows that team members *want* their coaches to be moral. Honesty truly is the best policy. Always treat your team members with equal respect and be straightforward in your communications. This is not a time to be coy. Your uprightness models the behavior you want from your players and sets the stage for the development of trust and honest relationships.

4. **Focus** – A great leader knows how to focus on the details that will lead both individual players and the whole team to success. As a coach you will eliminate everything but the key items your players need in order to make progress toward your mutual vision for the future. You will train your focus and that of your players on these few things.

5. **Supportiveness** – People give their best performances when they feel safe, heard, and valued. For example, if a team member fears being punished for "snitching" he may hold back important information about another player's dishonesty. Advocate for your players' trust by emphasizing your support of their honesty and straightforwardness. Your team members will train and play at their maximum effectiveness when they are confident you will back them up in their honest pursuits.

6. **Emphasize Clarity** – In a team situation it is essential for you to be clear on what needs to be done, in terms of both team and individual development. If you are at all vague in the way you communicate and implement your plans, your players will become confused about their own priorities. A sustained fogginess about your role as coach will breed confusion, discouragement and distrust. With clarity of communication you will be able to rally your team around your vision and your strategies, ultimately increasing your chances for success as a team.

7. **Believe** – When you are confident that your team members can accomplish anything, they probably will. Confidence is contagious. If you consistently portray that you trust them to get the job done, your players will be likely to take ownership of their own success and they may well surprise you with their progress. So, banish your fears and trust your players' abilities to learn and grow; remember what caused you to choose them in the first place and trust your own good instincts.

8. **Collaborate** - Do not be afraid to seek out the feedback and advice of others. You may have a great idea, but as a coach it will take a whole team of leaders to massage it into a plan that will turn the world upside down!. Just as a movie needs a whole host of people to bring it to life, so you need the contributions of your team, staff, and local community if you hope to succeed. Just as the point man on your team relies on and works with the rest of the team to score and win, so you need the contributions of everyone, players as well as staff, to successfully manage all you are in charge of, from a single game to a winning season.

9. **Develop Your Communication Skills** – Effective leaders are great communicators. They ensure that every team member is fully equipped with the information necessary to make the entire venture succeed. Good leaders establish and zealously guard a two-way communication channel between each member, as well as with themselves.

10. **Tackle the Tough Decisions** – A good leader must be willing and able to make difficult decisions in high-pressure situations. Your team members will look to you whenever a tough decision needs to be made. Be careful to ensure you have the whole picture before making your decision. Don't hesitate to request input from others, but remember the ultimate choice belongs to you. Once you've made your choice, don't change your mind or second-guess yourself. Step out and face whatever consequences may come.

Your Good Name

As a leader, you will be emulated in your community, so be careful what you do. It's only natural for us to want to become like those around us. Just as small children emulate their parents' behavior, people of all ages often want to be like a person they admire. Resist the pull to become like others of lesser standards; instead, let others become like you. Only be doubly-sure that you'll like what you see when they do.

Obviously, you should not commit any crimes or otherwise engage in illegal activity. Beyond that, everything you do can become a positive example for others to follow. Choose a lifestyle that enables you to be generous with your time. Allow yourself space to respond to those in need and to surprise people with kindness. Look for ways to affirm and encourage others.

Give of your resources. Give money to meet genuine needs. Give gifts, not randomly but thoughtfully, in order to refresh others. A good way to judge whether your actions will reflect positively on you is to ask yourself, "How will I feel if I see other people imitating me?"

Boost Your Reputation

Your reputation is largely a function of your lifestyle and actions. However, there are some character aspects you can build in your life that will over time develop how you are perceived by others. Here are some of the foundations for a good reputation:

- Do as you say you will (be careful what you promise, but keep your promises).

- Acknowledge it when you make a mistake; apologize and make restitution where possible.

- Respect everybody, including their opinions, strengths, and weaknesses.

- Respect individuals equally – do not play favorites.

- Have a clear set of values and act consistently with them.

- Encourage and build others up (do not cut them down).

- Act selflessly, setting aside your preferences to serve others as they need to be served.

Follow The Leaders

Some of the best coaches in history have lived by these values. Here are just a few:

- **Vince Lombardi** is one of the most well-known football coaches in history, most famous for his coaching of the Green Bay Packers. Under his guidance the Packers won a total of five National Football Championships, all within seven years and three of them consecutively. When he graduated from college, the Great Depression was making it hard for anybody to find a job, and the newly minted coach was no exception. After a long, hard search however, Vince eventually landed an assistant coaching job.

Lombardi later moved on to coach at West Point, where his unique coaching style emerged, a style based on execution and perseverance. After a brief stint with the New York Giants, he moved on to The Green Bay Packers, transforming them from the worst team in the league to the best.

Coach Lombardi held his players to the highest of standards, requiring them to participate in intense training sessions. When he incurred his first and only loss, he simply told his team, "This will never happen again," and it didn't. He simply refused to accept failure as an option.

- **Joe Paterno** was the head coach of Penn State's Nitanny Lions from the late 60s until 2011. Under his coaching, five undefeated teams won 24 out of 35 major bowl games. He was the first coach to win each of the four major bowls as well as two national championships. The team has won the Big Ten championship three times.

Coach Paterno was inducted into the College Football Hall of Fame in 2007. He was a great role model and an active participant in his community, contributing billions of dollars toward Penn State and its various departments.

Joe Paterno is a great model of perseverance. After incurring a sideline injury during a game against Wisconsin, he continued to coach his team through the 2007 Outback Bowl as he recovered. He was reinjured soon thereafter, but that didn't stop him; Paterno continued to coach his team from a wheelchair.

- **Red Auerbach** is the well-known coach of the Capitols, the Blackhawks, and the Celtics. During his coaching career he won 938 games and within ten years clinched nine NBA championships. While he served as general manager for the Celtics, he led them to win seven additional titles, making them one of the most successful sports teams in North America.

Auerbach was considered a pioneer of basketball; he focused on team play, defense, and a new offensive strategy called "the fast break." He made history by drafting the first African Americans in professional basketball. Many of the athletes who played under him have since been inducted into the Basketball Hall of Fame.

Red Auerbach has passed on his wisdom to thousands through his books on basketball and coaching. Today he is respected as a highly effective mentor, having worked closely with Bill Russell, Tom Heinsohn, K.C. Jones, and Bill Sharman. What truly made Auerbach a memorable leader is that he valued his players for their talents and motivation rather than judging them by their skin color or personality.

- **Bill Fitch** is a former NBA coach known for helping failing teams turn around. He transformed the Cleveland Cavaliers, the Boston Celtics, the Houston Rockets, the New Jersey Nets and the Los Angeles Clippers. In 2004, Fitch was ranked fifth out of all NBA coaches for all-time victories. He was named NBA Coach of the Year when he coached the Celtics and again as coach for the Rockets . In 1981, he guided the Celtics to the NBA Championships. Bill Fitch was named one of the Top ten greatest NBA coaches of all-time in 1996.

Coach Yourself to Good Health

The final and most important part about being an effective leader and coach is that you must keep yourself physically fit and healthy. When you're in shape you find it's easier to think positively and focus. You also set a positive example for others to emulate. The best way to protect your physical health is to eat a proper diet and to exercise consistently.

Diet – The first step is to staying healthy is to understand what a healthy diet really means. A healthy diet should include a variety of whole grains, fruits and vegetables, meat, poultry, fish, nuts, eggs, milk, yogurt and cheese. Fats and sugars should have a limited presence in your diet.

A good way to establish balance and variety as the hallmarks of your diet is to create an eating plan. To build an eating plan, first decide how many meals you plan to eat per day, how many snacks, and how much time you have to devote to eating, as well as planning and preparing meals. With time and experimentation, you can consistently build a healthy eating plan that steers you away from sugar and pre-packaged foods (that have who-knows-how-many toxic chemicals added) and toward fresh ingredients in easy-to-make meals and snacks that provide you with the nutrients you need to function at your best.

Exercise – The ingredient for a healthy life is to develop an exercise plan that will help maintain your fit body. There are many exercise programs out there, but if you're just looking to be healthy overall, engaging in some basic cardio fitness exercises, some foundational strength training, and stretching exercises will help you maintain your fitness level.

Cardio training activities may include walking, jogging, swimming, running, rowing, biking, jumping rope or hiking, to name a few. Aim for 20 minutes of cardio training, at least three times a week.

Strength training will help build muscles, burn fat and boost your metabolism. Simple strength training exercises include sit-ups, push-ups, pull-ups, weightlifting, resistance band training, and yoga. Some specific exercises as well as help planning your personal workout routine will be provided further on in this book, in the context of instructing your athletes in proper physical preparation.

For more in-depth, detailed information about leadership and your health, you can consult my two other books, Leadership: The Top 100 Ways to Be a Great Leader and Ultimate Health Secrets, where you can find additional tips, secrets, strategies, and ideas for bringing yourself up to peak performance levels.

Chapter 2: Form a Winning Team

To become a winning coach you must know how to form a winning team. A sports team can only be successful when everyone, including the coach, works together to win. Not only does teamwork help bring a team to victory, it also boosts morale and confidence, builds cooperation, increases social skills and trains players to take responsibility for their actions. These attributes are important for all areas of life, not just sports, and will help your players grow as successful individuals as well as top-notch athletes.

Creating Synergy

As coach, it is your job to create and bring your team together for a powerful burst of **synergy**. Synergy is when "the sum of the whole is greater than the sum of the parts." In terms of sports teams, it means that when each of the team members combines talents and skills, the team's success rate will be greatly enhanced. To achieve synergy, you must carefully match players with positions that reflect their greatest strengths. Your players must have the right attitudes for their strengths to be effective. When you recruit players to your team, you must be able to analyze whether or not they can bring the skills you need along with them. Sometimes it's a matter of recruiting players when you can see specific potential you can develop to meet a specific need in your team.

If you need to recruit someone to fill a particular position, you may not find the perfect fit in a fully developed player. This is where your coaching abilities will be most important. In this case it is more important to find somebody who has the right attitude than to find a star player. A willingness to learn and grow is most important; everything else is a matter of training.

A positive attitude is important. A winning team always displays a positive attitude. As the coach, one of your most important tasks is to model and encourage a can-do positivity among your players. This will, in turn, make it easier for your players to sustain positive relationships with each other.

Building Relationships

Successful relationships between team members helps foster team morale and often leads to solid relationships outside the team. Most team relationships form naturally in the process of working together, but some will take work on your part. As the leader, it is up to you to set the tone of your relationships with the team. If you model respect, openness, and approachability to your team, the team members will by and large follow your lead.
It's also essential that the members of your team each have a clear understanding of what you expect from them as well as what they can expect from you . Make sure that your team knows you are accountable, reliable and responsible. If you

do not follow through on your commitments, your team will lose respect for you and question your true intentions.

Focus on praising your team for positive accomplishments instead on pointing out mistakes. Give verbal praise when players have accomplished a goal or task that has pushed them out of their comfort zone . Don't hold back from giving out constructive criticism, because that is what helps your team improve. Just make sure you do it in a non-threatening manner. You don't want your team members to feel attacked or belittled, but accepted and safe. If your players are confident that you only have their best interests at heart, they will feel safe enough to receive anything you say.

Supportiveness Exercise

Gather your team members together in a meeting or a casual gathering. Put one player in the "hot seat" and ask everyone else to take turns identifying one positive skill or personality trait they have seen in this individual. After each person has had a turn, put another player in the hot seat and continue this exercise until all players have had the opportunity to receive from the others. As coach, you also get to participate in naming a strength of each player.

While it is your job to be able to recognize and maximize the strengths of your team members, the truth is that your players will see different things than you see. You may not realize that one of your players is super-organized or another consistently steps up to the plate when leadership is needed, but another player might have noticed. This supportiveness exercise can offer fresh insights into the players. All the while it will help build positive relationships and can both reinforce your team's cohesiveness and boost its confidence.

Always listen well to your team members and encourage your players to do the same for their peers. Listening and hearing are two different things. When you hear, your ears are simply registering sounds, but active listening involves your entire being, body, mind and soul. You are listening with a purpose: to be able to help the other player grow and develop, both as a person and as an athlete.

Finding the Best Players for Your Team

Recruiting is a large part of being a coach; you are responsible for finding players to fill your team. to be a winning team your goal is to find the best mix of players possible. No matter how many candidates there are to choose from, you need to know what to look for in a prospective player.

All in all, you should look for players who are skilled in the sport you're coaching, are established in the fundamentals of the game, and who can mentally connect with the game. Since you won't always find the perfect candidate, you want to be confident at the very least that those you select have a teachable and positive attitude. Here are a few more items to look for in a player:

- **A Good Ball Handler** – The first thing you'll want to look for is the prospective player's ball-handling skills. The best way to determine this is to request several full-game tapes (not highlight reels, which won't show enough of the player's overall performance). Watch how the prospective player pursues the ball, blocks, and executes passes. Analyze the player's offensive and defensive strategies. Take notes on what you can see from the game tapes in terms of the player's strengths and deficiencies. Be sure to note any exceptional abilities, as well as how well you think you can repair the player's deficiencies through coaching.

- **Room to Grow** – Does the prospective player have the potential to physically transition to the next level of play? For example, a prospective football player who has already maxed out in terms of physical strength only has growth potential if his size matches up with the position you need him to fill. If you're looking to fill a quarterback position, for example, you will want a player who has or can build arm strength and who already has explosiveness, hip fluidity, the ability to change directions, and top speed. Look for sport-specific and position-specific attributes to identify the best players.

- **A Good Match** - You're also looking for a player who can mentally connect both with the sport and the rest of the team. Every team naturally establishes its own identity, an identity that is often different from what the public sees. You'll want to have a good feel for how a prospective player will mesh with your existing team's dynamics. For example, if your team consists of hard workers who keep pushing to improve and your prospective player is well-known and popular in his present team, he may be resting on his laurels and might never have known the necessity of hard work. Your prospect may be unaware that he has a ways to grow before he'll be able to match the caliber of play at this level of the game. In either case you'll need to decide if a little coaching will be all that's needed to set your player on the right path, or if you'd be better to take a pass on this individual.

- **A Responsible Academic** - If you're a college recruiter, you'll need to know a player is disciplined enough to keep his grades up. You want to find recruits who have good enough grades to maintain sports eligibility. Most students are able to keep up their grades and continue to play sports. In this respect, as a college recruiter, the best time to start looking seriously is when the students are high school seniors.

The Fine Art Of Recruiting

Recruiting is hardly an exact science; it requires a lot of hard work, a huge dose of people-savvy and high risk tolerance in order to land a successful batch of players. Of course your players will not all be the same. Frankly, you want it that way. Research has shown that heterogeneous teams, i.e., a group of people who think and respond differently from each other, in the end become much more productive than teams made up of people who all think alike.

Some players will fit easily into almost any environment and thrive there, while others need some time to adjust to all the changes thrown at them before you'll see them perform at their best.. Some players may not be the most skilled ball handlers on your team, but because they mesh well with the team's dynamics they may flourish and develop skills beyond more talented players who don't mesh as readily. Hopefully you'll be able to establish a team with a balanced mixture of skills, personality, and adaptability.

Recruiting can be incredibly time-consuming. If you're new to coaching it'll feel like you're drowning in game tapes, interviewing an never-ending stream of prospective players, and it'll feel like you're taking forever to make decisions. However, the longer you're a coach, the easier it will become. You will eventually know exactly what to look for and you'll more than likely end up creating a vetting system that works for both you and your players.

Where to Find Prospective Players

Depending on the level of sports you're coaching, there are several strategies that coaches use to find recruits. Coaches often fill Pop Warner, high school, and lower age-level teams by advertising in schools and around the community. At this level, holding try-outs will likely give you what you need in order to put together a team.

The college recruitment process is more complicated. For one thing, player recruitment is a two-way street. Most colleges start looking for prospective recruits when they are in their final two years of high school. They usually do this by sending representatives to different high schools once or twice a year, but it is important to be aware that students with true potential may be the ones reaching out to you.

Students who are really serious about playing college-level sports may well take the initiative to contact you through email, by calling, or by joining your affiliated recruitment networks. Some potential recruits will also send you an introductory video. Therefore, it is important to make it easy for recruits to reach you. The more you can get your contact information out into the secondary school environment, the better your chances. You should also take steps to be highly accessible on social networks, especially Facebook and Twitter. You will want to leave your contact information with online recruiting networks as well as with high school coaching staff and school counselors.

Athletic Team-Building Tactics

Team-building strategies are crucial for any organized sport. They help individual players build strong interpersonal bonds that help them work smoothly together. The way team members communicate and interact can greatly enhance the performance of the entire team, so it is important that your players grow together into a functional unit.

Goal-setting

The most critical of your team-building strategies is to establish a clear, common goal. The obvious objective in any sport is to win the next game, but the best way to get there is for everyone even remotely connected to the team to be working toward an overarching goal. The goal for your organization will reflect your values and your coaching priorities. When your overarching goal is clearly outlined, it helps to ensure that everyone is on the same page. There will be fewer conflicting voices, greater unity and, ultimately, greater synergy across the board.

Even though you're the leader, you want the team's supportive goals to belong to the team. If at all possible, include the whole team in the development of objectives that will move it toward your overarching goal. If the players can see the need for a certain objective, if they claim ownership, they will be much more likely to invest the necessary effort to see it reached.

Use your overarching goal as the compass for all you do for and with your team. Plan your practices and team activities to push toward the team's supportive goals. Evaluate every idea, proposal, and suggestion by how effectively it promotes your overarching goal.

Help your team stay committed to the goal. State and re-state it often. Point out to the team members, before beginning a specific drill, how it contributes to their pursuit of the big-picture objective.

Coach Each Position

It is also important for each team member to be clear on the responsibilities inherent to his position. Assigning players to positions that showcase their strengths will contribute to the effectiveness of the whole team, but players also need to know what is *not* their responsibility. If, for example, everyone chases after the ball, leaving nobody around to play defense, then you've got a recipe for disaster on your hands. Each player must know at all times where he needs to be and what he should be doing.

Promote Trust and Cooperation

One way to deepen interpersonal relationships is to pair team members together as partners to build a strong **support system** for each individual. When your players have a strong support system, everything runs smoother. Encourage them to discuss their personal goals with their partner and share obstacles they are facing. In addition to providing perspective and opening the door to peer advice, these relationships can promote accountability to the team's objectives.

Build Inter-dependence and Cooperation

I suggest you use the following activity early in the season to help your team bond and learn to work together to solve problems. The **knot circle** can be a lot of fun while, at the same time, strengthening cooperation. Have your team stand in a circle. Ask everyone to shut their eyes, reach across the group with their right hands, and grasp another player's hand. Then ask them to do the same with their left hands, making sure they grab somebody else's hand. Once everyone has both hands connected, have let them open their eyes. Their next task is to untangle themselves without letting go of anyone's hand. This will require them to work together to solve a problem that affects them all.

Promote Personal Development

Building positive values is another important task of a coach. As players participate in their sport, it is important to reinforce things like:

- The value of hard work

- The importance of fairness

- How to follow rules

- How to treat others with respect

- How to respond when treated unfairly

Many sports teams participate in community events, fundraisers and other volunteer opportunities. These give players opportunities to expand their **social skills** as they are encounter a variety of social situations. It broadens their horizons, giving them a glimpse of life from a variety of perspectives and helps them begin to view themselves as contributors to their community at large. They develop as persons, not just as players.

Define your Team Ethics

Building strong **team ethics** is also important for the daily functioning of your team. Negative emotions such as fear and distrust easily arise during the early formation of most teams. At this critical juncture, the way you respond and how you teach your players to respond to each other will set the tone for the entire year, for better or for worse. As a coach, it is important that you model team ethics from day one. Your practice of these ethics is critical, since your players will follow your life long before they respond to your words. Your words, however, are essential. It is equally important for you to "coach" your team in living according to your ethics.

Not only should your team ethics be spoken, they should also be written down, posted, and distributed to the entire organization – players and staff included. As you write up your **team ethics statement**, here are some aspects to consider:

- Integrity
- Equality
- Respect
- Responsibility
- Diversity
- Courage
- Dependability

Define each word in simple, clear terms, so the players can see exactly how it applies to their own words, deeds, and values.

Promote Self-belief

Encourage players to develop a strong sense of **self-belief**. It is important that some of their confidence and motivation be self-driven. That being said, it is important for you to encourage an "iron sharpens iron" culture. Let your team members encourage and learn from one another.

It is equally important for you to model self-belief. Always present a positive attitude toward yourself and extend that attitude toward everyone you meet. Leave yourself open to both encouragement and "sharpening" from both staff and from your players.

Avoid ridicule like the plague! Any form of derision can destroy the trust you've worked so hard to build and can tear down your hard-won culture of mutual growth. Any time you're tempted to speak negatively to a person, it's an indication that all is not right inside. In that case, I recommend you hold your tongue and first deal with your own inability to accept yourself. Only then will you be able to speak Truth in a way that heals and promotes peace.

Adjust to Team Stages

There are several "stages of team development" according to Psychologist Bruce Tuckman, labeled "forming, storming, norming, performing" and later, "disbanding." Each stage marks a unique way of interacting and presents specific challenges to both members and leaders. As a coach, it will help you to recognize which stage your team is in at any given time so you can help your players function effectively and continue to grow into the next stage.

The **forming** stage is when the members of a team meet each other for the first time. There are often negative emotions like fear, distrust and discomfort swirling inside players' heads during this time. In this stage, it is the responsibility of the coach to introduce elements that will reduce the team's uneasiness. You can do this by finding common ground on which the team can come together and by providing a clear structure in terms of an overarching goal, activities scheduling, and expectations.

The **storming** stage marks the transition from individual players into an actual team. At this stage, ideally, players begin to learn from one another. This increased level of interaction can also generate conflict. You may discover that suddenly your team consists of a bunch of people with large egos who don't can't seem to agree with anyone's ideas. As a coach, it is your responsibility to serve as mediator during this stage. Your job is to encourage individuals to communicate their thoughts and feelings to each other, and to respectfully listen to the opinions, ideas, and feelings of their teammates. When conflicts arise, it is your job to work with the various parties to come up with workable solutions so that the team can move on to the next stage.

The **norming** stage occurs when your team settles into and begins to work as a team. Your players finally accept and embrace their roles as a valued contributor to the team. Identities and roles are acknowledged. The new normal becomes firmly established. As a coach, you will probably not have to do much during this stage except to work alongside your team to keep the good times rolling.

Then there is the **performing** stage. Your team begins to seriously make progress. Members function in ultimate synergy with each other and are able to – as a team – effectively find their way through obstacles and challenges. During this stage, it is up to you to strategically delegate tasks. You want to keep each player functioning in his "sweet spot" as much as possible. This is the time to provide feedback to team members so they can sharpen their skills. Motivate your players and reward generously them during this stage. You now know your team well, so you will know what will motivate each individual and how to fire up your whole team.

Inevitably, the team will at some point move into the **disbanding** stage. We're talking the end of the season or the end of the year, in athletic terms. The only risk with this stage is that some team members may fear change. As the coach however, you are responsible for encouraging players to embrace their future.

You become the diplomat who smoothes over the inevitable and makes the process as painless as possible.

Core Values

Throughout their life as a team, you will be tasked with instilling core values into your players. These values can help turn your team into a productive powerhouse, because they stand for success and progress. They are easy to remember because they all start with the letter "C."

- **Communication** – As the coach, you must communicate to your team about their roles and give them feedback as to how they are doing. Without adequate and appropriate communication, your team will be unable to make progress.

- **Control** – As the coach, you have the authority for every aspect of your team. Your players have control over their work but that work is subject to your oversight. Never forget this.

- **Creativity** – As the leader, it is up to you to encourage and foster creativity. Teams that are creative often have more opportunities and ideas to work with. Creativity can enhance group communication as everyone builds off the ideas of everyone else.

- **Competence** – As the coach, you are responsible for preparing and helping your team to adequately complete the tasks given them. When you see gaps in competence it is up to you to implement strategies to fill those gaps by training, discussion, etc.

- **Collaboration** – Collaboration is a powerful resource when used correctly. As the leader, it is up to you to promote friendly collaboration and to mediate any conflicts that arise. Collaboration goes hand-in-hand with creativity.

- **Clarity** – As the coach, part of your job is to ensure that your team understands the concept of teamwork as well as the goal they are working toward.

- **Commitment** – A team that is committed works well together and is in sync with each other. As the coach, it is up to you to encourage commitment as one of the core values of the team.

- **"See" ahead.** – Coaches who think a few steps ahead in the game are often those whose teams cross the finish line first. Such foresight can help you stay on top of the competition. When you can think of strategies first and adjust quickly your opponents' strategies, you will be more likely to seal the win. Teaching this to your team can increase your advantage.

You can discover additional team-building tactics and more in my other book, Team Building: Discover How To Easily Build And Manage Winning Teams.

Chapter 3: Prepare Them Physically

Athletes must be physically prepared if they want to be successful. For sports, physical preparation consists of basic things like physical fitness, sports nutrition, and sleep. Your practices should target your players' speed, mobility, flexibility, strength and ability to change tactics on a dime. Most sports require stamina, energy and a body that can withstand all of the rigors of an extended game. As a coach, it is your job to assist your players in their physical preparation, even as you keep yourself in shape for the rigors of coaching.

Sports Nutrition
The first step in physical fitness is nutrition. You want your players to know how to maintain a healthy diet that will prime them for peak performance. The energy your players need to compete will come from what they eat and drink. The greatest energy-laden nutrients for any athlete are **carbohydrates**, **proteins**, and **fats.**

Carbohydrates

Carbohydrates are the main energy source for athletes. Carbs provide the necessary nutrients for muscle use, making them suitable for any sport. One gram of carbohydrates provides four calories of energy.

There are two types of carbohydrates: **simple** and **complex**. Simple carbs are a quick source, because your body can absorb and convert them quickly into usable energy. Complex carbs take longer for your body to digest. When carbohydrates enter your body, they are broken down into glucose, fructose and galactose. These are the sugars your body converts into the energy you can use on the field. Unused glucose gets stored in your liver and your muscles as glycogen. When your body can no longer store extra glucose, it gets turned into fat. **Glycogens** are important because they provide your body with energy you can use to fuel your workouts. Any short, intense movements like sprints or lifting weights are fueled by glycogen.

The second main reason that carbohydrates are important is because the right amount will prevent your body from using protein as energy. The main job of protein is to help your body build bone and muscle tissue, so if your body relies on protein for energy, your ability to develop muscles and build healthy bones may decrease. Excessive protein consumption can also put extra stress on your kidneys, causing them to work extra hard to break down protein byproducts.

Where can you find natural sources of carbohydrates? Simple carbohydrates can be found in fruits, vegetables, sports drinks, white bread, pasta and packaged cereals. Complex carbohydrates reside in starches, dry beans, whole grains, the seeds and skins of raw fruits and vegetables, nuts, and seeds.

Protein

Protein is another important component of your body. It is made of amino acids, which help build your muscles, bones, skin, hair and tendons. Protein supports enzyme production and the transportation of nutrients through your body.

There are over 10,000 different types of protein in your body. However, it is hard for your body to store protein. This means you need to ingest a healthy amount of protein each day . The best source for protein is through natural food sources like meat, eggs, fish, nuts, fruits, and vegetables. Protein is important for athletes because it helps rebuild muscle tissue damaged during exercise and games. A typical adult needs 0.8 grams of protein for every kilogram of body weight. If strength training, athletes require 1.8 grams per kilogram of body weight. An endurance athlete will need 1.4 grams per kilogram of body weight.

Here are some of the best sources of protein:

- Eggs
- Peanut Butter
- Fish
- Chicken
- Cheese
- Yogurt
- Turkey
- Beef
- Tofu

Fats

Fats are the third building block of essential sports nutrition. While fats have a notorious reputation for causing health problems, they are actually helpful and necessary for proper nutrition.

There are three different types of fats: **saturated**, **unsaturated**, and **trans-fats**. Saturated fats are found in meat, eggs, cheese, yogurt, milk and butter. They can cause health problems if consumed in excess. Unsaturated fats are found in plant sources such as olive oil, canola oil, fish, flaxseed and avocados. they are considered healthy fats because they can actually help lower your cholesterol levels and reduce your risk of developing heart disease. Trans-fats are similar to saturated fats and should likewise be avoided.

Fats provide your body with the highest concentration of energy. They can help you perform sustained and low-intensity movements, such as walking. However, it is important that athletes carefully monitor fat consumption, because fats take a long time to digest.

A Balanced Diet

While it is important to provide your body with these specific nutrients, the easiest way to ensure the proper nutrition is to eat a balanced diet full of variety. We'll start with the food pyramid. According to the food pyramid, a balanced diet should be half filled by fruits and vegetables. The rest should be split between protein sources (beans, nuts, fish, chicken, lean red meat) and whole grains. Healthy fats and dairy products are fine in small quantities. Sugar and potatoes, should be minimized. Water especially, but also coffee, and tea (with minimal sugar) should be drunk throughout the day to sustain proper hydration.

Next, we need to talk about breakfast. Breakfast is the most important meal of the day because it jump-starts your body with the nutrients and energy necessary to run for the rest of the day. This is especially true for athletes. The best breakfast will contains energizing foods such as eggs, whole grain oatmeal, bran cereal, quinoa, and peanut butter. Another great way to start the day is with a nutrition-packed smoothie.

Another key strategy is to keep the body energized by eating multiple smaller meals throughout the day instead of the standard breakfast, lunch, and dinner. This strategy works well because it keeps athletes full from morning to night. The best energy-rich foods for lunch and dinner include brown rice, sweet potatoes, lean pork, lean beef, seafood, skinless chicken, beans, sauerkraut and vegetables. The best snacks include fruits, peanut butter, yogurt and dark chocolate.

Energy Supplements

Another option to physically prepare your players for competition is to encourage the use of nutritional supplements. Supplements are useful if you have a vitamin deficiency or if you have an aversion or an allergy to some of the "healthy" foods. I recommend you consult a doctor when you are considering their use. Here are some of the most popular, all-natural energy supplements:

Biotin (Vitamin B7)

Biotin is important for your body because it helps your body metabolize fat and carbohydrates. Biotin deficiencies are known to cause diseases of the skin, the nervous system, and the intestinal tract. Our bodies will not work well without this vitamin. Type 2 diabetics benefit from biotin, because it helps to balance blood glucose levels. Biotin can also help prevent birth defects and can improve the quality of your hair and nails. A typical adult body generally needs 30 mcg of biotin a day. Foods that contain biotin include fortified cereal, barley, milk, soy, egg yolks, fish, chicken, broccoli, pork, and spinach.

Licorice Root

Licorice root is my favorite naturally energizing supplement; it has worked the best when I need an extra boost of energy throughout the day. Studies have shown that licorice root boosts energy levels by helping the body regulate stress-inducing hormones. I like licorice root because it sells for a reasonable price, it is a natural product, and it gives me consistent results without negative side-effects. You can swallow the capsules or you can break them open and add the powder to a cup of tea or water.

Copper

Copper helps your body create red blood cells. It can also help prevent osteoporosis and promote proper functioning of your heart. **Copper deficiencies can trigger chronic diarrhea and fatigue.** A typical, healthy adult needs 900 mcg of copper each day. Good food sources for copper include shellfish, vegetables, and whole grains.

Oat Straw Extract

Oat straw extract is a natural substance that helps the heart pump more blood to your brain, which provides a steady stream of alert energy throughout the day. You can sprinkle it on your food, mix this into your juice or tea or ingest it as a pill. If you often feel tired in the morning, this product may work well for you. I have noticed a considerable boost in my morning energy levels since I started using oat straw extract.

Iodine

Iodine supports the functioning of your thyroid, which in turn generates the essential hormones that help regulate other major organs . It helps your thyroid gland regulate your body temperature. Deficiencies in iodine can lead to thyroid underactivity, weight gain, and increased colds. A typical, healthy adult needs 150 mcg of iodine each day. Good foods to eat for iodine include iodized salt (but be careful not to overload on salt), dairy products, seaweed, kelp, fish, and canned tuna.

Rhodiola

Rhodiola is a great natural supplement to take if you find yourself feeling sluggish in the afternoon. This substance helps duplicate the molecules in the body that give us energy.

Manganese

Manganese is important because it can help metabolize fats and carbohydrates as well as stimulating the growth of bones and connective tissue. It can also help protect your body against free radicals. Manganese can help protect your body from the ravages of osteoporosis, arthritis, and diabetes. A typical, healthy adult needs between 1.8 and 2.3 milligrams of manganese each day. The best foods to eat for manganese include pineapple, nuts and seeds, oats, unrefined cereals, and wheat germ.

Multivitamins

Multivitamins offer a balanced source of energy support in a single pill. Most multivitamins contain all the essential vitamins, minerals, and amino acids that our bodies need for balanced health and energy.

Important warning: many multivitamins labeled specifically for energy contain caffeine. If you're looking to avoid this stimulant, read the labels carefully.

Zinc

Zinc is important for your body because it can help boost your immune system. It can help preserve your vision and can help your wounds heal more quickly. Deficiencies in zinc can lead to skin rashes, weight loss, hair loss, and depression. A typical, healthy adult needs 15 milligrams of zinc each day. Vegetarians will typically need to supplement their diets with zinc because this metal is primarily obtained by eating meat. In addition to meat, zinc can be found in nuts, seeds and leafy greens.

Ginseng

Ginseng is a natural, plant-based herb that grows in Asia and North America. Ginseng is best known for boosting the immune system and lowering sugar levels in the blood. Recently–released studies that have reported that ginseng boosted the energy of cancer patients as effectively as cancer-free individuals.

Vitamin B

As you already know from our discussion on energy super-foods, B vitamins are important to boosting energy levels. Although we can get some B vitamins through the foods we eat, supplements can make up the difference, especially for people who test deficient. Vitamin B-12 is also well known as an energy booster.

Amino Acids

Amino acids help your body stay energized throughout the day—without them, your energy will drain right out from under you. Amino acids are generously available in protein-rich foods. They can also be obtained in supplement form

Bee Pollen

Bees collect pollen as a part of their honey-generating activities. it contains of all the nutrients that the human body needs. 40% of bee pollen is protein while the rest is made up of amino acids and B vitamins. Bee pollen is great for building stamina and burning energy.

Spirulina

Spirulina is a plant that thrives in water. It has a texture similar to seaweed and is related to algae. Spirulina is an excellent source of protein; it can be eaten as a plant or in capsule form

Gotu Kola

Gotu Kola is a natural substance used for centuries by people in countries like China and India to improve mental focus. It comes from a plant and does not contain any caffeine. If you often suffer from stress and anxiety, gotu kola may be able to help you relax and clear the fog from your head.

Omega-3 Fatty Acids

Omega 3-fatty acids also help your body stay energized. The best way to get this substance is to eat seafood. If, however, you are allergic or have an aversion to seafood, you can still get what you need elsewhere. Two cups of mixed salad greens will satisfy your daily requirement. Another source, flaxseed, will meet your omega-3 requirements in only four tablespoons. It can be sprinkled on almost anything.

Sleep

Sleep is another important element of physical preparation. Not only is sleep important to your athletes' sustained health, it enables them to perform at their best. Most training programs, whether established by coaches or the athletes themselves, include scheduled rest days. Just remember that a rest day is not a substitute for a good night's sleep.

Studies show that even one night without quality sleep can greatly reduce athletic performance. Sleep-deprived athletes don't metabolize glucose as well as a rested athlete, causing their bodies to produce higher levels of cortisol. An overload of cortisol can result in poor memory, resistance to insulin, and a longer recovery time from injuries. A less-than-quality night's sleep can also lead to lower levels of the hormone leptin, which assists your body in regulating hunger and body fat storage.

The best way to get a good night's sleep is to develop a pre-bed ritual that you follow every night. Most importantly, encourage your players to go to bed and wake up at the same times each day. This will program their bodies to expect a set number of hours of sleep at night and to use those hours most effectively. Most adults in the prime of their lives require eight hours of sleep, optimally. Alcohol and caffeine can disrupt a sleep schedule if taken too close to bedtime. If you normally drink alcohol or coffee, stop drinking caffeinated beverages and anything alcoholic two to three days before a competition.

The next best thing you can do to ensure a good night's sleep is to expose your body to plenty of light in the morning, but to lower the lights as you approach bedtime. Light helps you feel awake and increases your mental alertness.

To maximize your exposure to natural light during the day:

- Eat your breakfast outside or near a window.
- Open your curtains to let in the light during the day.
- Take your work breaks either outside or in a location where you can look outdoors (it is also good for your eyes to be able to look for long distances)
- Take a short walk outside on your lunch break.
- When you buy your next car, consider looking for one with a sun roof.

At night, there are many ways you can reduce your exposure to light:

- Lower the brightness on your computer and television screens.
- Wean yourself away from all electronic screens thirty minutes before bedtime.
- Wear yellow-tinted sunglasses (yes indoors) to block the blue light that tells your body clock to stay awake.
- wear an eye mask to bed.
- Replace bright illumination with nightlights at bedtime. Subdued lighting will avoid triggering a false wake-up call, if you need to get up in the middle of the night.

De-stress

One thing that can cause restlessness at night is stress or anxiety. To reduce stress levels, encourage your athletes to practice deep breathing, meditation and visualization.

When you lay down at night, close your eyes and visualize a peaceful and calming scene; this will help you relax and peacefully float off to sleep. Some people find it helpful to listen to soft background music, or recorded sounds of nature.

Sleep is essential for your body to repair itself. Approach sleep not as a loss of productive time, but as a gift to yourself, a gift of nourishing kindness and restoration.

Stretching and Workouts

Encourage your players to set up and maintain a regular workout schedule. Stretching strengthens muscle flexibility, which can reduce chances of injury. Workouts help keep athletes' bodies in tip-top shape throughout the season. Remind your players to stretch after their muscles are somewhat warmed up, in order to avoid injuring themselves, also to stretch gently at the end of a workout to enhance long-term flexibility.

The difficult part of a person's workout is that no single program works for everybody. An effective workout depends on the sport one is training for, as well as other biological factors such as age or prior injury. What follows are some general instructions you can pass on to your team to get the season started well.

The first step to set up a workout routine is the planning stage. While it may be as time-consuming as a workout itself, it'll be worth the one-time commitment. Follow these steps and you'll be on your way to implementing your own workout routine in no time:

- **Schedule** time to work out. Unfortunately, you cannot just work out whenever you find yourself bored and/or faced with spare time. A workout routine must be consistent, even if you are limited to only a few times weekly. A typical athletic schedule consists of three days a week with one day of rest in between workouts.

    Scheduling may be helped by the use of a reminder tool. If you have a generally set schedule throughout the week, it can be fairly simple to pencil in consistent workout times. However, if you have a life that requires varied work hours , you can still make it a goal to work out at least three days a week. You'll just need to plan around your week's work schedule.

    Provide yourself with clear reminders. This stage should be easy. If you use an online calendar you can easily schedule workout times for several months ahead, setting electronic reminders. Most smart phones come equipped with calendars that can alert you before your workouts.

If you use a manual system, attach your workout times to a triggering event that occurs regularly. If you work out after work, use the end of the work day as your trigger to head to your workout spot. If you work out first thing in the morning, set your workout clothes out the night before, placing them in a prominent spot where you'll see them first thing when you wake up.

- **Be accountable** for your workout goals. It is easy to set goals but harder to actually pursue them. If it's hard for you to kick yourself into action, find an accountability partner who will. Most coaches will hold their athletes accountable for performing their workouts, but players can also ask a team member to serve as their accountability partner.

- **Be realistic** when creating your workout plan. Many hardcore athletes will get up at 4 am to catch a 5 am workout, but if you're not an early riser this is never going to happen. Choose a workout schedule that is workable in *your* life. If you have to work out in the middle of the day or in the evening, that's perfectly fine.

- **Add variety** to your plan. Doing the same old routine on the same old days can get boring – and that's no lie. When you get bored, you often feel tempted to start skipping. Give your workout routine some variety. Work different muscles on different days. Do strength training one week and cardio the next. Mix it up and try out some yoga. Do strength exercises in week three as opposed to week one. You get the picture. A varied workout routine will keep you interested for much longer.

The second step in creating a workout routine is know what parts of your body and what type of training you actually need to do. While all athletes are different, there is a common rule of thumb you can use to physically prepare yourself as an athlete. Most athletes train for **explosiveness, functional strength, endurance, balance, flexibility** and **agility** by focusing on **core muscles**, particularly the back, hamstrings and glutes.

Certain sports require special types of training. For sport-specific workouts, you can check out my sports books: Football, Tennis, Swimming, Soccer, Baseball, Golf and Basketball.

Common **explosiveness** exercises include plate jumps, frog squat jumps, box squat jumps, dumbbell jumps, finger cleans ravers, dumbbell jerks, long box jumps and concentric box jumps. Popular **endurance** exercises include cardio activities such as walking, jogging, swimming, running and dancing. **Balance** exercises usually consist of arm raises, triceps extensions, leg extensions, side leg raises, hamstring curls and bicep curls. **Agility** exercises include figure runs, sprint lateral shuffles, box drills, ladder drills, cone drills and balloon drills.

When I was younger, I was an amazing athlete and although I no longer compete, I still try to maintain my body just as an athlete would. I personally break up my workout routine into four sections. One day I will do legs, another day arms, another day chest/back, and then finish off with shoulders. I follow this schedule regularly. Typically, I will take one to three days off between workouts, depending on my life schedule and how I'm feeling.

In my younger days, I loved to use heavy weights, push my limits, and see just how big and strong I could get. It was quite exciting, and I got some great results. Arnold Schwarzenegger was one of my role models. However, now that I have entered my 40s, I have adopted a different strategy, using lighter weights and greater repetitions to reduce my chances of getting injured. I don't sport the super-defined muscles that I used to have, but my current routine has given me a lean, muscular physique that is still very powerful and more than adequate for daily living.

My Strength Training Routine

Leg Day: I will do a short walk around the block or jump on a mini-trampoline to warm up my legs. I then stretch out my quadriceps, hamstrings, and calf muscles. When properly stretched, I will start off with 25 squats just using my body weight. I go nearly all the way to the ground and I ensure that I consistently use good form.

I use a Bowflex Revolution, which mimics many of the major exercise machines in a gym. I do lightweight leg extensions next until my legs are burning. After a short rest of a minute or so, I move on to hamstring curls with light weights and around fifteen repetitions. The last exercise will be calf raises. I like to stand on a curb or similar object and just use my calf muscles to lift up my body weight. This completes one full set of all my leg exercises.

I then repeat the set but this time, now that I am warmed up, I push myself harder to complete even more repetitions. After a brief rest I will complete at least one more set and, if I feel like pushing myself, then I will do a complete fourth and fifth set as well. If you are working to build power and strength, then after the first warm up set, you will want to add some weight and cut back on the repetitions.

Arm Day: On this day I work out my biceps, triceps, forearms, and grip strength. After stretching out my arms, I will take some lightweight, dumbbells and perform arm curls with them until I feel a nice burn. I will then take an even lighter dumbbell for the next exercise, the triceps kickback.

Following that, I work out my forearms and do wrist curls with a dumbbell. I then take a grip strength ball and squeeze it in my hands till I got a nice burn. The final exercise is the triceps push down.

I will typically do a few extra sets of arm curls at the end of the routine, since I'm doing two separate triceps exercises. As with all strength training routines, the first set is for warm-up, and you really want to push yourself on the additional sets.

Chest/Back Day: I start off by stretching my chest and back. I will then take some dumbbells and simulate a bench press motion. When my chest muscles are feeling a bit tired, I end the set with dumbbell flies.

I then move to a back exercise, called upright rows, using a dumbbell with this as well. Following this, I perform cable crossovers on my Bowflex Revolution. Then I move on to seated rowing.

After this, I do lower back hyper-extensions, then some sit-ups, and finish the first set with push-ups. Chest and back day is typically one of the tougher workouts.

Shoulder Day: I start off by stretching out my shoulders. This routine is done exclusively with lightweight free weight dumbbells. I begin with Arnold presses, take a rest, then perform rear lateral dumbbell raises followed by lateral dumbbell raises and frontal dumbbell raises. I then pick up some heavier dumbbells for shoulder shrugs to work my trapezius muscles. As usual, I take a short rest between each exercise.

There a few other things to keep in mind when working out. You can exercise your abs and lower back every day, along with your calves. You can exercise your neck muscles daily as well, and it is good to do various motions with your neck to relieve stress and increase strength. It is also a good idea to eat a protein shake or another healthy high-protein food fifteen to thirty minutes after you have completed your workout.

Stretch Yourself

Finally, you'll want to come up with a good stretching routine that you can use at the end of your workout. Your stretching routine should take about 15 minutes. Not only does stretching help maintain and increase flexibility, it can increase your range of motion, relax your mind, and help increase your circulation. Here are some basic stretches you can incorporate into your stretching cool-down routines:

Standing Reach-Up Quad Stretch – This stretch targets your quadriceps. Stand tall and take one step forward. Reach both arms up and push your hips forward. Lean back and then away from your back leg.

Arm Swings – Stand straight with your arms out at your sides, parallel to the floor. Slowly swing your right arm forward and rotate your torso to the left. Return to the original position and continue the rotation to the right, then back to center. Do this continuously for 30 seconds.

Split Stance Side Lean – This stretch also targets your spine rotation. Begin in a split stance with your left leg forward. Holding your hands behind your head, bend your upper body to the left and then raise back up. Bend to left 10 times and then repeat to the right.

Chest Stretches – Stand tall with your feet slightly wider apart than your shoulders. Extend your arms out from your sides, keeping your palms facing forward. Stretch your arms back as far as you can until you feel the stretch; then hold for a few seconds and release.

Rotating Stomach Stretch – This stretch targets your abdominal muscles. Lie down on your stomach and bend your arms, placing your hands palm-down near your shoulders. Straighten your arms and push your upper body up off the floor, while your hips remain on the ground. Gently bend your left elbow, lowering your left shoulder toward the ground and slightly twisting your spine. Straighten your left arm and repeat the process with your right arm.

Trunk Rotations – Stand with your feet shoulder-distance apart. Put your hands on your hips and slightly bend your knees. Keeping your feet firmly planted, slowly rotate your upper body from side to side, without turning your hips or knees.

Wall Lat Stretch – This stretch targets your back muscles which can help your jumping strength. Stand facing a wall, three feet back from it. Lean forward, keeping your body in a straight line, until you can place your palms on the wall. Use your right foot to take a step back, placing your heel against the floor. Drop your head between your arms, then return your right foot to its original spot and raise your head. Repeat 10 times with each leg.

Shoulder Stretches - Stand straight, with your feet a little wider than your shoulders. Relax your knees. Swing your right arm straight across your chest, using your left arm to pull it toward you. Feel the stretch in your shoulder. Repeat this stretch with your left arm.

Ball Quad Stretch – This stretch works your hip flexors and quads, which can help improve hip mobility, sprinting and direction change. Stand upright with your feet together. Place a small ball between your knees and squeeze as you use your right hand to pull your right ankle up to your butt and hold it there for 25 seconds. You can position your left hand on your leg for stability. Repeat, using the left ankle.

Hamstring Stretch – Lie on your back. Loop a towel under the sole of your right foot. Pulling on the ends of the towel with both hands, raise your leg until you feel it stretch. Return to your original position. Do this stretch 10 times for each leg.

Shoulder Stretch – This stretch targets your shoulder muscles. Stand straight and put your right hand on your left shoulder. Put your left hand on your right elbow and pull it toward your left shoulder until you feel the stretch in the right arm. Hold for 20 seconds and then repeat with your left hand on your right shoulder.

Bicep Stretches - Stand straight, with your feet slightly more than shoulder width apart. Keep your knees slightly bent. Hold your arms straight down at your sides with your palms facing forward. Stretch your arms back as far as you can until you feel the stretch in your biceps.

Toe Touches – Stand with your feet spread widely apart. Stretch your right arm as far as you can toward your left toe. Repeat for the other side. Alternate sides for 10 repetitions.

Triceps Stretch - Stand straight with your feet slightly more than shoulder width apart. Keep your knees slightly bent. Bring both hands above your hand and then reach them down to your mid spine. Feel the stretch in your triceps as well as your shoulder.

Side Stretches – Stand with your feet aligned with your shoulders. Keeping your chest straight, lean to one side. Avoid twisting in either direction. Hold the stretch for two seconds and then repeat for the opposite side. Do this stretch in sets of 10 repetitions.

Upper Back Stretches - Stand upright with your feet slightly more than shoulder width apart. Keep your knees slightly bent. Lace your fingers together and pull your hands away from your body, with your palms facing outward. You should feel your upper back begin to loosen up and stretch between your shoulders.

Back Stretches – Lie on your back. Bend your knees and pull them to your chest. Fold your hands under the backs of your knees. Roll forward and allow your feet to touch the floor. Then roll back until your head nearly touches the floor. Do this stretch for a set of 10 repetitions.

Calf Stretches – Position yourself in front of a wall or stable surface. Put one foot forward and lean against the wall, using your palms for support. Make sure they are aligned with your shoulders. Place one leg straight away from the wall as you keep your other leg bent. Feel the stretch in your calf. Repeat with the opposite leg.

Split Stance Spine Rotation – This stretch targets your spine rotation and can help you change directions quickly. Begin in a split stance with your right leg forward and your hands behind your head. Rotate your upper body to the right and then come back. Rotate to the right 10 times and then repeat to the left.

Groin Stretches – Sit tall on the floor. Press the bottoms of your feet together. Gently hold your ankles and slowly lower your knees toward the ground. Feel the stretch in your groin and thighs.

Avoid Overtraining

Training under a weekly schedule is important but you must know the importance of your body's limits to avoid **overtraining**. Overtraining is when you train beyond your body's ability to recover. Many athletes make the mistake of overtraining, especially when they are nearing a competition, because they believe it can make them stronger and more unstoppable. However, overtraining can actually hinder one's performance and athletic abilities. It can also lead to injuries. Rest and recovery are crucial for becoming a top-performing athlete.

It is quite easy to figure out if you're overtraining. Other than conscious awareness that you're pushing yourself too far, the symptoms of overtraining include:

- Feelings of fatigue and tiredness, lack of energy
- Aches, pains and soreness in your muscles and joints
- Decline in performance
- Restlessness, unable to sleep at night
- Headaches
- Decreased immune system
- Irritability
- Depression
- Loss of passion for sports
- Decreased appetite

There are several ways to catch yourself heading toward overtraining before it becomes a problem. First, you can watch and track your heart rate. Write down your heart rate after doing several different intensity levels of workouts. If you see that your heart rate begins to decline or that your resting heart rate starts to increase, it is likely a sign that you are heading into overtraining.

I suggest you use the **orthostatic heart rate test,** developed by Heikki Rusko, to test for overtraining:

- Pick a time to lay down and rest for 10 minutes. (Use the same time each time you test.)

- Record your heart rate at the end of the 10 minutes.

- Stand up, wait for 15 seconds to elapse and measure your heart rate again.

- Continue to track the elapsed time, measuring your heart rate at the 90-second mark and again at the end of 120 seconds.

- Athletes who are *not* headed toward overtraining will show a consistent heart rate over the course of 120 seconds.

- If your heart rate shows an increase of 10 beats per minute or more, you are overtraining and should cut back.

Another way to avoid overtraining is to maintain a training log where you track not only what you did each day but how you feel at that time. From your entries over time you can pick up on trends that you might otherwise overlook. For instance, if you notice increased discouragement with your progress or even boredom, it might be time to ease up on your training for a couple weeks.

Your teammates are another resource to rely on if you wonder whether you are exercising too much. It is often easier for outsiders to see objectively, so ask your peers to let you know if they see negative changes in you. There will be plenty time for you to return the favor in the future.

The best way to avoid overtraining altogether is to see that your body gets enough recovery time and adequate hydration. Always give yourself at least 24 hours of rest in-between workout sessions. A sports massage may help you relax mentally and can help reduce both physical and emotional stress. Drink water before, during, and after training sessions. It's especially important to drink plenty of water following a massage; you need the extra liquid inside to help flush out all the toxins that were loosened up.

Recovering from overtraining can take weeks, so it's best to avoid this in the first place!

For specific health and energy strategies, you can find more valuable information in my books, [Ultimate Health Secrets](#) and [Ultimate Energy](#). In them you can learn how to design your personal diet plan, how to keep your energy up, and how to stay in overall great shape.

Chapter 4: Prepare Them Mentally To Compete

In the competitive environment of sports, mental preparation is just as important as physical conditioning. You can have the world's best health and the ideal physique for athletics, but without the right mindset, all your training won't be worth a hill of beans. A strong, positive attitude isn't just important for success in sports; it can mark the difference between failure and achievement in all areas of life.

Athletes who are mentally strong are able to recover from performance errors, they can manage their anxiety, surmount stress, and sustain their focus without being distracted from their objectives. Mentally strong athletes are not devastated by setbacks. They are self-starting problem-solvers who are able to view their sports performance as just one facet of life as a whole.

Learn to Set and Achieve Goals

Without goal-setting, athletes are unlikely to achieve success. An athlete's goals provide a focal point for his efforts. Without a clear objective, an athlete is more likely to veer off-course; while he may accomplish a few good things, the overall direction of his life is less effective than it could be if he had focused most of his energies toward a single end. As a coach, a good portion of your work in player development will revolve around helping athletes set, plan toward, and reach goals. Here are some of the activities you will want to include in your developmental coaching:

Teach Goal Development. Without a vision, people run amok; so said a man who knew what he was talking about. As coach, it's your job to establish an overall vision for the whole team. By so doing you build a framework around which your individual players can structure their personal goals. You also model goal-setting for your players. Here are some practical how-tos for goal setting that you can apply to yourself and pass on to your team:

- Brainstorm for 30 seconds about what is most important for you to accomplish this year (or this season). Without evaluating anything, scribble notes of everything that comes to mind. After thirty seconds, scan what you wrote, looking for common themes; you want to group the possible selections into clumps of related ideas. Then rank those ideas by what has the most potential to do the most good. Select no more than four to focus on. If your selections all fit under a single heading, all the better.

- Write down your goals. This may sound trite, but just the act of putting them down in black and white (or any color you prefer) will solidify your goals and make them more "real" to you. Writing them down marks your commitment to focus on these few things.

- Frame your goals in positive terms. I suggest starting each goal with the phrase, "I will easily..." to give yourself a psychological burst of positive thinking. It may sound goofy or pretentious at first, but the more often you repeat these phrases, the more your mind will accept them as reality and the easier it will become to let yourself achieve your goal.

- Formulate your goals so that you will know when you've reached them. They must be both measureable (how fast will you run? By when?) and achievable (a stretch for you but not beyond the realm of the possibility).

- Review your goals every day, several times a day. Post them prominently wherever you'll see them; remind yourself that these are what you're working toward. Speak your goals out loud to yourself when you first wake up. Repeat them to yourself before you drop off to sleep.

Encourage Goal Development

Give your players opportunities to tell their teammates about their goals during practice sessions. If necessary, encourage them to select goals that are compelling and will really excite them. Too many people set small goals that lack passion. Tell your players to not be afraid to dream big and shoot for something truly incredible. Once they know what their goals are, the next thing to do is to help them develop an action plan.

Plan toward your goals. Having goals is great but if athletes don't know how to work toward them, they are likely to never reach them. Let's say an athlete's goal is to increase her upper body strength. She's got her goal—now she has to think about her action plan and write down the specifics of scheduling and training objectives. The advice of a trainer would also help provide specific activities and exercises to reach the stated goal.

Again, encourage your athlete to read her goals and review her action plan daily. This will sustain proper focus on her goals and will feed her motivation . Let your athletes know that whenever they feel unmotivated, they should refer back to their goals and action plans.

Know your "why." Encourage your athletes to question why they want to be on your team, why they want to play. Remind them that it has to be *their* "why" – not their mother's, not their father's, not because they've always played and they have nothing better to do with their time. This is akin to learning why you want to get out of bed in the morning or answering the eternal question: "Why am I here?"

No, I'm not trying to get all existential on you. The truth is, if your players have an internal motivation, they will work ten times harder than if they were just working to please you, the coach. They need to figure out why their goals matter to *them*.

If they are not sure why they set goals, they may not feel very motivated when times get tough. They need to know their purpose, for their own sake, not just for the sake of the game. For a powerful object lesson in the importance of knowing your "why," do an internet search on the phrase "comedy is what I do" and watch Michael Jr's explanation.

A person's "why" may not be all that profound. Some people give their whole lives to sports because they because they enjoy it. For them, that is the ultimate motivation. Some are motivated by the opportunity to grow as a leader. Others love the feeling they get when they've worked together with a team to accomplish something great. The key, however, is finding that "why." When your players tap into *that*, almost nothing can stop them.

Affirmations

Affirmations are encouraging statements you can use to jump-start your motivation or stir up your enthusiasm when it begins to fizzle. They are easy to create and you can use them any time you need to realign your focus, your thinking, your beliefs, and your attitudes.

I suggest you teach your players to follow these steps to create and use their own affirmative statements:

Start with your goal statements. Reword the most basic goal statements as if they have already been accomplished. For example, if your goal is to learn to dribble a basketball equally well with both hands by the end of the season, you could turn it into a statement of affirmation by saying, "I easily dribble the ball around my opponents using either hand."

Include statements of energy and attitude, as well as statements of skill. A sample energy statement would be, "I have more than enough energy to participate fully in everything I will encounter today." A sample attitude statement would be something like, "I love my life and am grateful for all I have been given."

Your objective in creating statements of affirmation is to help your inner being begin to believe in your capability to be a slightly enhanced version of yourself. Go ahead, take those things you want most to achieve and turn them into positive statements as if you have already achieved them. It may feel like you are lying to yourself at first, but you aren't; you are just looking into the future at what you fully anticipate to happen. You are clearing away any vestiges of doubt as to whether or not you are able to accomplish this. You are fully committing in the deepest part of your being to seeing yourself develop to match your deepest desires.

The professionals who count such things say that we should repeat our statements of affirmation at least 200 times a day. At least that's what they say it will take to counteract all the negative, degrading, doubt-producing statements we've heard over all the years of our lives. We also need the repetition to counter all the negative naysaying messages we hear around and the limiting phrases we – out of old habit – keep saying to ourselves.

I don't know if you're willing to commit to that level of repetition, but anything you can do will be an improvement over your old ways of thinking. Personally, I prefer to attach them to specific triggering actions. I repeat them while I'm getting ready in the morning. I repeat them when I get in the car to go somewhere. I repeat them when I break for lunch, and again before I go to sleep. I encourage you choose a specific activity and let that activity trigger the repetition of your affirming statements.

It's also important to write down your statements of affirmation. Just as it's important to write down your goals, the act of putting them down on paper will make them more real to you. They also provide a visual reminder. You need at least one copy to post in a prominent place, somewhere you will see them daily and be reminded to repeat them. Keep a copy on three-by-five cards, and carry them with you in pocket, purse, or billfold. I you prefer, you can put them on your phone or do whatever else places them at your fingertips for immediate review.

Most importantly, speak your affirmations aloud. What you say out loud lodges in a different part of your brain when you can hear yourself saying the words and use your facial muscles to speak them. Even if you are in a public place where you can't speak out loud you can always say them silently, moving your lips to form the words.

Positive Self-Talk and Visualization

Positive self-talk is another powerful mental strategy. It is the process of replacing all the negative, limiting, shaming, and belittling messages that are in our heads with positive, empowering, enabling, and confident phrases. It's not enough merely to banish negative thinking. This would leave a vacuum that would soon be refilled with new negative, cutting, and destructive thoughts. No, with this practice you are going to replace those negative messages with much more powerful positive truth-telling.

An example of positive self-talk is when an athlete says, "I am strong and fast enough to win this game." However, positive self-talk isn't just saying good things about yourself to yourself. The first step is to identify our negative self-targeted statements. It's very easy for us to be critical of ourselves. Things like, "I am so slow," or "I will never win," slam the door on hope. Tackling our negative internal messages is essential; our thoughts and beliefs are the source of all our actions. I suppose you've heard the statement, "Whether you think you can or you can't, you're right." Well, it's true.

The first step to eliminating negative self-talk is to become aware of it. This is a process that takes time. Some people are so used to hearing negative thoughts that they aren't even aware of them. However, over time you can become increasingly tuned into negative thoughts when they arise. One dead give-away is when you hear the phrase, "I can't" or "I will never," coming out of your mouth. It's easy enough to replace these thoughts with corresponding positive statements. Just replace the negative with its positive flipside, starting your statement with the phrase, "I will easily..." Since you already have an arsenal of affirming statement, pull out one to swallow up the negative thought. Repeat it enough times and it will start to feel more real than whatever you dread.

The second step is to utilize visualization. If you think you can't do something, visualize yourself doing it anyway. Walk yourself through every detail of successfully completing whatever it was that your silly negative thinker said you can't do. Research shows that when you consistently visualize yourself accomplishing a task, you will become strongly inclined to achieve it.

Finally, if you're bombarded by a slew of negative nasty messages, a helpful strategy is to focus on one of your best and happiest memories. Sometimes just thinking of you at your happiest can banish fear, doubt, and insecurity and paint yourself in a positive light. It can build a positive space in which to start building positive alternatives.

The Recall Exercise

The recall exercise helps athletes build up a strong positive frame of mind. by reflecting upon two separate events from their own lives.

First, ask them to recall a game in which they were wildly successful. As they visualize each moment of the successful event, ask them to look for key things they did or thought that may have contributed to their success. Were they highly focused? Super-coordinated? Quicker to respond than usual? What were they able to do beyond their normal capabilities? In what ways were their interactions with teammates a contributing factor?

Remind the players that the things they identified represent emerging skills and growth in character. Encourage them to consider how well these things reflect existing goals and desires. These are qualities that athletes could focus on to progress to the next level of play.

For the second phase of this exercise, ask your players to recall a game where everything seemed go wrong. Using this example, ask them to identify key difficulties they had, both in performance and in attitude that may have detracted from a successful game. What negative self-messages came into play? What failures to perform? What emotions were predominant? How did these emotions impact their ability to play well? These things all represent possibilities for improvement, both in attitude and performance.

Sustain a Positive Attitude

Athletes with an overall positive attitude are more likely to win. Attitude is a choice; athletes who choose a positive attitude will be the ones who succeed. A good way to identify athletes who have a positive attitude is to see which ones view the sport as a way to challenge themselves to grow. They view performance failures as an opportunity to learn. Athletes with a positive attitude focus more on excellence than on perfection and readily admit that nobody is perfect. They also tend to show respect toward coaches, other team members, and themselves.

Strengthen Self-Motivation

Without self-motivation, athletes may find it hard to put effort into their game. Successful athletes are cognizant of the benefits they gain from winning and being on top. Instead of losing heart, this only increases their motivation to win. Self-motivated individuals are able to pursue their goals on the field, even when the benefits are not directly in front of them. They recognize that the benefits they receive stem from their participation in the sport, more than from the outcome of any individual game.

If an athlete is in need of self-motivation, ask what is his "why" for playing. If he doesn't already know, this can trigger an honest and thoughtful reflection of his values, desires and deep motivations. If the player knows his "why," use that to help him focus on what really matters.

Develop Powerful Social/Communication Skills

Athletics require a great deal of socialization and communication, not just within the team but off the court. When athletes realize that they are just a small part of a whole organization bent on winning, it can be a powerful motivator. This may boost their mental game as they work to avoid letting down their coaches, team members, communities or families. To achieve team synergy it is important for athletes to communicate their thoughts and feelings to their teammates and their coaches.

Part of communication is listening. Athletes need to be able to actively listen – and not just hear – what others are saying. Developing powerful social and communication skills can help athletes improve their ability to deal with conflict, face difficult opponents, assist team members, and handle other challenging situations.

Manage Anxiety

It is normal for athletes to feel anxious before a big competition. However, when athletes don't effectively manage their nervousness and anxiety, it can sabotage their performance. Successful athletes practice deep breathing exercises or meditation as they prepare for the game. They often perform pre- and post-game rituals to help manage their emotions. They learn to accept anxiety as a part of the sport and even recognize its energy as an added boost that can actually help them play better. Successful athletes do not let anxiety get in the way of their mental readiness or dampen the intensity of the fire in their bellies.

Here is an effective deep breathing exercise that can not only reduce anxiety but also reduce pain, increase energy levels, improve circulation and regulate blood pressure:

> Step 1: Position yourself comfortably. If possible, lie flat on your back.
>
> Step 2: Slowly and deeply breathe in through your nostrils.
>
> Step 3: As you inhale, let your stomach rise. As you exhale, let it fall.
>
> Step 4: Once you've gotten the hang of step 3, begin inhaling fully, so your entire lungs fill with air, expanding into your abdominal region as well as the area below your shoulders.
>
> Step 5: Exhale and let the air flow out of you like a deflating balloon. Try to stay as relaxed as possible. As your exhalation is almost complete, contract your abdominal muscles, squeezing all the air from your lungs. Rest a moment in this state.

Take several of these breaths both before and after competition to transition yourself into a relaxed, calm and ready state.

Ritual Suggestions

Here are a few more ideas your players can choose from as they build their rituals:

Before the game:

- Eat a meal at a pre-planned time.
- Double-check your equipment.

- Visualize your success.
- Scope out the venue you'll be playing in.
- Wear clothes that make you feel great.
- Play back recordings of your best games.
- Spend some time alone in a quiet place.

During breaks in the action:

- Sit back for a moment and enjoy the game; soak in the fun of it all.
- Find something to do to occupy your mind and distract yourself from any internal negative emotions or external tension.
- Visualize your success.
- Speak with your coach.
- Review your goals and speak your positive affirmations back to yourself.
- Talk with other players who are positive-minded and supportive.

Contingency Planning

Since most sports are intensive and high-impact, it is important for coaches to have contingency plans in the event of an injury or an otherwise unexpected event. Pre-planning for unexpected events can condition players and coaches to think on their feet, preventing drops in performance due to the distraction of change.

There are all sorts of unexpected scenarios that can occur, from a sudden player injury to losing your team equipment at the airport. The best way to face unplanned events is to have a staff back-up plan that will keep the players focused and calm while staff works behind the scenes to resolve the problem. Both players and coaches can learn to be prepared to face any situation, even the unexpected.

Player Injuries

For coaches, the most common scenario requiring a player adjustment is when a player gets injured before a big game. Player injuries usually occur during a warm-up session. When this happens, it can generate panic in coaches and players alike. This panic, however, can be minimized by having a contingency plan in place.

When a player incurs an injury, the first thing you should do , after ensuring that the player is taken care of, is to assess your available players and pick a replacement. You can actually write up a potential player substitution grid in advance and keep it hidden deep in your clipboard. Hopefully you won't need it, but if an injury crops up you will have already thought this through and prepared viable options beforehand.

If the injured player is one of your best, challenge an up-and-coming first-string player to take on the position, then fill his former place with someone lower down in the ranks.

As the leader, you must remain calm and composed throughout an injury situation.. Do not display any negative emotions that may be flooding your mind, but focus instead on communicating your confidence in the replacement player and the rest of the team. A pre-game motivational speech can challenge all your players to up their game and can enlist their cooperation in smoothing over the adjustment and in affirming trust in the replacement player(s).

Expect Surprises

Don't you just love it when your opponents surprise you with a powerful counter to your strategies? I know your first reaction is to panic, but let me encourage you to think of this as a good thing. It means that your offense was working. Now all you have to do is adjust your strategy to counter their counter to your...well, you get the picture. It's a simple exercise in problem solving, and that's what you're good at, right? Now, dig deep and think up a way to render the opposing team's strategy ineffective.

Your greatest advantage in this case is to have equipped your players beforehand to quickly adjust to changes in both roles and strategies. See if you can shift positions and functions to effectively combat your opponent's strategy. If that doesn't work, try something else. Don't forget to enlist your players in looking for weaknesses on the other team that you can exploit to your advantage.

Of course, there is never a guarantee that you'll blow the other team away with your tactic. If your players are ultimately unable to find a way to defeat an opponent's surprise strategy, hold a team discussion after the game as to why they were unsuccessful and what they can learn from the experience to better manage the next surprise on the field.

Of course, the variety of surprise scenarios coaches may encounter are endless. Since these events are typically unforeseen, it is a good idea to keep training yourself to strategize and think creatively under pressure. As a coach, you too can use sudden events, whether failures or successes, as a chance to become even sharper mentally and more effective.

The key in most high-pressure situations is to stay calm. If you panic, your players will too, and good luck recovering then! Better to set aside your emotions and focus on getting your players into an improved position.

Coaches also must occasionally face challenging situations within their team. Common difficulties may include panicking during competition, inconsistent use of a newly learned technique, personal problems that players are unable to leave off the field, or an outburst of emotions when players disagree with an official's call.

Here's some advice I've found effective to share with players, as the situation warrants:

What if you freeze during a game?

- Imagine yourself in your perfect game; take a deep breath and then rejoin the **present** game, imagining it to be your perfect game scenario. This will help you relax and play at your best.

- Promise yourself some time after the game to face your outside problems. Then promise yourself to do the best you can in the current game and turn your attention back to the needs of the moment.

- Practice the deep breathing exercise I mentioned earlier and use that as a means of relaxing yourself. Alternatively, you can use your positive affirmations to move yourself back into a productive mental state.

Your Players Struggle to Master a New Strategy

- Remind yourself that a change often takes some time and that almost nobody masters a new technique immediately. Give yourself permission to be human; be content to continue in a learning state.

- Exercise patience and persistence – tell yourself how this technique will greatly improve your playing ability.

- Discuss with your coach why the new technique isn't coming easily to you. Your coach may be able to identify the source of your difficulty.

- Take a break and don't burn yourself out.

- Try changing your playing environment, if such a thing is possible. For example, you may do better on an inside court than an outside court.

Your Team is Under-prepared

- Tell yourself that you've gotten the bad performance out of your system and that now you're ready to do your best.

- Reassess the event and pick out all of the positive aspects.

It is all the more important under these circumstances to communicate to your players that you are confident in them and in their abilities. Don't act as if you expect to lose, because they may surprise you, and then wouldn't you look the fool?

Boost Team Morale

Team morale is important for winning because without it, your players may become less energized, less motivated and sloppier. It can also become a cause for injuries from less-than-alert players taking the field.

Low team morale can stem from an increase in pressure before a competition, losing a player, hanging around a negative player or any number of negative situations. As a coach, one of your jobs is to keep your team morale high and address it immediately when you see morale slipping. While you are unable to control individual situations, you can foster a productive, safe, and positive environment, which can have a major impact on your players.

There are many simple yet powerful ways to boost your team's morale; the best thing is that most of them are simple. For example, simply saying "good job" or giving a specific compliment when a player does something positive can have a big impact. Celebrating small successes along the way can also help keep players in good spirits. When players go on for weeks, months or years without hearing positive feedback, it can make them feel as if they are not doing well enough, or are not a valuable member of the team. In addition, compliment the team as a whole when you see them working hard or sacrificing for the good of the team. Ours is not a generous or grateful society as a whole, so your players need to receive genuine affirmations to tell them that they are noticed and valued.

As you know, setting goals is a very important part of reaching success, but sometimes the daily slog can become tiresome for your players. To keep them in a winning mindset, try setting "fun" goals to lighten up the mood. These may be silly and meaningless but are lighthearted and a good source of stress-relieving laughter. Everyone needs to have some fun, even serious athletes. For example, you could have a contest to see which player(s) can find the craziest sports news story or see who can stay awake the longest on a road trip.

Schedule Down Time

Athletes can easily get wrapped up in their pursuit of excellence. Coaches, too, can get busy and forget that athletes have lives outside of the game. When a player spends too much time away from home, friends and family, it is not a good thing. To counteract this tendency, as you build your practice schedules and plan training to build toward games, with adequate down time. Talk to your players about their availability and preferences so you can ensure you're giving them a good balance between sports and the rest of life.

Skill Sharing

The great thing about being part of a team is that your players bring a diverse set of skills to the table. One player may be great at ball handling, while another is a skilled defender. To affirm your players' strengths and sustain team morale I suggest hosting a skill-sharing session periodically.

Choose one player and ask him (hopefully a little in advance) to give a brief workshop on a specific skill. First, put the player through his ball-handling paces so all the team can see his expertise, then turn him loose to build up his teammates' skills. Give the players time to interact, socialize, and learn from one another. This can help players gain the respect of their peers, deepen their friendships and improve their skills at the same time.

Open Door Policy

Your players need to know they have your ear. While it is essential that you have some down-time, too, your team should feel welcome to approach you. When your door is open, it needs to be consistently welcoming. In case of emergency, players need to know that you want to hear from them.

Even when you make attempts to maintain high team morale, it is still possible for your players to feel down and frustrated. After all, athletes are only human. If your morale-boosting tactics don't seem to work, face the problem head on. Invite your players to tell you about what is bothering them. Elicit their feedback on their coaching needs.

Pump 'em Up With Word Pictures

Motivational speeches and pep talks have proven useful in boosting the mental game of your players before they begin competition. Most coaches give these speeches in the locker room or on the sidelines of the game. Motivational speeches help capture your players' attention and get them in a winning mood. The most effective pep talks include a visually powerful statement, story or metaphor. Unite the team with a reminder of a past victory, build up their sense teamwork, underscoring how team dynamics are especially essential for that day's competition.

Your speech should paint a vision of success and facilitate positive expectations. Use key events to fire up their motivation such as, "Imagine; if we win this competition today we will be the first team from our city to win the championship in 10 years!" Try to avoid passive speech and use plenty of action words. Wrap up your speech with a clear call to action, one that can be immediately implemented when players enter the game.

Here are some examples of real-life motivational speeches on YouTube. Pay attention to how they are structured, and listen for positive, action-invoking language that is used:

- Ray Lewis Greatest Motivational Speech of All Time by Charmcity187

- Win At All Costs – Sports Motivational Speech For Champions by Team Fearless

- NOTHING WILL STOP ME – Motivational Video 2016 by MotivationGrid

Building Your Best Team

Your strongest foundational strategy is to build the best, most powerful team you can. You will do this by maximizing on each player's talents and skills and strategically positioning your players for the greatest effect. If you are starting out with an all new team this will take some time and experimentation, as you get to know your players. If you have been working with the same players for a while, structuring an optimal team should be a little easier, but it will require the same amount of care. Here is a tool you can use to help define your team.

1. Create a list in three columns, one for the player's name, followed by his strengths and, in the third column, his weaknesses. Fill in this list with each player's attributes. An interesting exercise after you've made your primary assessment, is to ask your players to tell you what *they* view as their greatest strengths and the skills in which they feel the least confident. Not only will you learn how well you know them, you will also get a sense of how well they know themselves.

2. Make up a second list containing each position on the team. Beside each position write the primary skill(s) required to play that position. This will serve as your template for making player assignments. Make several copies of this template.

3. Fill in a copy of your template, matching each position with the player whose skills and body type best match the position requirements. This is just a start. Actually, you may want to work on a white board first, shifting players around until you've found a workable solution.

4. As you uncover new strengths or see a player's skills developing, you may want to adjust the positions to give individuals a chance to test how far they can grow in a different direction.

5. Your template can also prove useful in planning for games, allowing you to strategically place your players opposite opponents they can effectively counter.

6. Use your template for contingency planning. For each position, assign at least one alternate player who is capable of filling in as needed. Keep this list handy so you can draw from it in case of emergency. It will allow you to easily adjust your team on the field to accommodate any situation.

7. Use your contingency plan in training. Your players need to be able to quickly adjust to changes in the team's makeup. Practice swapping out players during scrimmage play, simulating real-life situations, and coaching players in making smooth adjustments.

Chapter 5: Prepare to Win

Winning Strategies

As you have seen thus far, physical and mental preparation are the most important factors in preparing yourself to be a winner. However, those are just the beginning. This last section will provide you with even more tips and strategies on how to help your players become winners in any competitive situation.

Push Beyond The Comfort Zone

Hold your players to the highest standards and teach them to expect the same of themselves. Burn into their minds:

- Commit to winning. Don't just hope that you'll win – tell yourself that you WILL win.

- Instead of expecting to fail, tell yourself over and over that failure is not an option. Your subconscious brain will soon begin to believe that you will win, thus boosting your chances of success.

- Keep striving to improve. Work to run faster, play harder and longer, etc.

Know the Game Rules

Most official sports come with a set of rules that all players must follow. Before each season, make sure that you're current on all of the rules. A mistake here can cost both you and your team dearly. It can disrupt your team's game performance and it might even cost you the game. It wouldn't hurt to set up an illegal situation and see how soon your players catch on.

Establish Yourself as a Resource

Teach your players to look to you and the rest of your staff as resources at their disposal. Encourage them to learn all they can from you and from other professionals, whether players or coaches.

Take Practices Seriously

Some athletes do not take their practices seriously and think it doesn't matter if they try their hardest. They are sadly mistaken Help your players understand that athletes who take each practice seriously and perform as if it were a real game are the ones more likely to come out as winners.

A famous coach once said, "Practice doesn't make perfect. Perfect practice makes perfect." Let your players know that you can tell when they are not giving their all. Then, when you see players wholeheartedly throwing everything into their work, praise them loudly.

Never Give Up

Remind your players to keep pushing to the very end. Point out that there has never been professional athlete who did not get where he is today without consistent determination and unwavering focus. Exhort them to hold on, even when they feel like throwing in the towel. When you can see energy flagging, urge players to speak out loud their positive affirmations, as a way to get themselves back in the game. If time permits, provide a break or a comic distraction that will let players' minds and emotions relax, rest, and recharge before diving into the fray once more.

Restore the Fun

If your players don't enjoy the game, their hearts will just not be into it. If their hearts aren't in it, They'll not put much effort into winning. Help your players rediscover the fun in the sport. Mix up the positions. Once in a while, bring a younger team to join you and mix them into your team to share a fun scrimmage.

To dial back the serious competitive nature and regain a sense of play, have your players handle the ball with their non-dominant hand for a change. This puts everyone at a disadvantage, and hilarious bloopers and accidents should have everyone laughing before long. Later, when you return to "serious" training, hopefully some of the spirit of fun will linger on.

Failure Does Not Equal Loss

It is crucial that athletes don't view losing as a failure or as something that lessens their personal value. If an athlete repeatedly views loss as a personal failure, it can become increasingly difficult to build a winning, positive mindset. Help your athletes view losses and mistakes as valuable opportunities to learn, grow, and work toward success.

You Can

Negativity is a strong emotion and it is, unfortunately, plentiful. Many people will try to tell you that you "can't" do or accomplish something, even as a coach. Athletes who want to be winners must tune out this type of negativity. Remind them to never allow anyone around them to tell them what they can and cannot do. Help them counter negative comments by speaking aloud what they know is a positive truth. Encourage them to avoid associating with anyone who brings negativity into their lives.

Overcoming Tiredness

Sometimes your players will feel like lazing around instead of practicing. Your challenge is to empathize with them without pandering to their desires. If you can reach them where they are at, you can then influence them to overcome their own reluctance and commit to working again. Of course, if the team doesn't respond to gentle persuasion, you can always wield your authority as coach to get them up and moving!

Encourage Self-development

Hold individual conferences periodically with each player. Use the time to encourage initiative-taking, goal-setting, and planning for personal development. The more individuals take responsibility for their own growth, the more they will mean business, both in practice and during games.

Organize

Organization is always a boost to anyone's chances for success. Athletes may just assume they don't need to be organized, thinking it's the coach's job. In that case they need to be taught that taking responsibility for their stuff is the mark of a mature individual.

In an academic setting the players who are most organized will be most likely to earn good grades. If you can help your players organize their academic lives, the self-discipline will seep into their training as well. Don't hesitate to bring in academic counselors or hold study skills seminars to underscore the value you place on academics.

Keep your eyes open for indications that students are suffering from lack of organization and discreetly do what you can to help them grow.

Encourage Mentorship

They say it takes a village to raise a child; it also takes a village to build a team. I'm sure you are all too aware of your own limitations; well, turn those limitations into an opportunity to model teamwork before your team. Welcome the contributions of other adults who can help your players grow. If one of your athletes is struggling with an issue that you know another player has successfully overcome, don't hesitate to get the two of them together for a problem-solving session. If your team just can't seem to hear what you're saying, don't be afraid to bring in another player or a visiting coach to get your point across. Sometimes another person can get through in a way you can't.

Extend an invitation to your students before they graduate to come back at any time in the future to encourage your players.

Inspire 'em!

Inspiration is contagious. Your own inspiration can help boost your players' confidence, self-motivation, and determination. So, where do you go for your inspiration? From other coaches, locally or industry-wide. Legendary coaches have arisen in all sports. One thing the best coaches have in common is their ability to inspire others. Here are two of the most inspirational coaches in the history of sports:

John Wooden

John Wooden is one of the best coaches in basketball. Between 1963 and 1975, Wooden coached the Bruins and led them to 10 NCAA Championships. Many believe that Wooden, in order to achieve these accomplishments, was solely focused on winning. However, this wasn't the case. Wooden's focus was on being an inspiration to his players – communicating a winning mindset to them. Wooden knew that his players would win those 10 championships as long as they had the right support system that would allow them to develop their abilities and skills.

During a speech to other coaches, Wooden once said, "You cannot find a player who ever played for me at UCLA that can tell you that he ever heard me mention "winning" a basketball game. He might say I inferred a little here and there, but I never mentioned winning. Yet the last thing that I told my players just prior to tip-off, before we would go on the floor, was, 'When the game is over, I want your head up, and I know of only one way for your head to be up. That's for you to know that you did your best. No one can do more. You made that effort.'"

Wooden is best known for focusing on excellence. He always held his players to high standards, expecting them to always give 100%. His vision went beyond just "winning" to building and fostering a winning mindset.

Phil Jackson

Next we go to a coach who sees the importance of both teamwork and spirituality. Phil Jackson once said, "Our society places such a high premium on individual achievement it's easy for players to get blinded by their own self-importance and lose a sense of interconnectedness, the essence of teamwork."

When Jackson led his team, the New York Knicks, to the 1973 NBA championships, a voice in his head helped him keep him focus during a victory party. Instead of celebrating the victory, Jackson aspired to keep his team going and training as if there had never been a victory. He simply pushed them to go "on to the next one." However, he always felt left with emptiness.

Because of that empty feeling, Jackson introduced his team to meditation and other focusing/calming techniques to help them live in tune with their team and become fully aware of their own playing abilities. He organized his practices so that every player handled the ball and they spent equal time on the court; he did not allow his top players to monopolize the limelight. Though this practice was met with much protest and strong skepticism at first, Coach Jackson slowly saw his team mesh and begin to act in synergy.

The 25 Best Coaching Quotes

1. "Failure is good. It's fertilizer. Everything I've learned about coaching, I've learned from making mistakes." – Rick Pitino

2. "Winning is not a sometime thing; it's an all-time thing. You don't win once in a while, you don't do things right once in a while, you do them right all the time. Winning is habit. Unfortunately, so is losing." – Vince Lombardi

3. "I think the most important thing about coaching is that you have to have a sense of confidence about what you're doing. You have to be a salesman, and you have to get your players, particularly your leaders, to believe in what you're trying to accomplish on the basketball floor." – Phil Jackson

4. "Most people get excited about games, but I've got to be excited about practice, because that's my classroom." – Pat Summitt

5. "I learned this about coaching: You don't have to explain victory and you can't explain defeat." – Darrell Royal

6. "Each person holds so much power within themselves that needs to be let out. Sometimes they just need a little nudge, a little direction, a little support, a little coaching, and the greatest things can happen." – Pete Carroll

7. "Selecting the right person for the right job is the largest part of coaching." – Phil Crosby

8. "I fell in love with coaching. I loved interacting with young people, having the opportunity to make a tremendous impression on them." – Morgan Wootten

9. "To be as good as it can be, a team has to buy into what you as the coach are doing. They have to feel you're a part of them and they're a part of you." – Bobby Knight

10. "Coaching is easy. Winning is the hard part." – Elgin Baylor

11. "You don't demand respect, you earn it." – Steve Seidler

12. "Coaching in the NBA is not easy. It's like a nervous breakdown with a paycheck." – Pat Williams

13. "Coaches have to watch for what they don't want to see and listen to what they don't want to hear." – John Madden

14. "Constant, gentle pressure is my preferred technique for leadership, guidance, and coaching." – Danny Meyer

15. "The [best] coaches… know that the job is to win… know that they must be decisive, that they must phase people through their organizations, and at the same time they are sensitive to the feelings, loyalties, and emotions that people have toward one another. If you don't have these feelings, I do not know how you can lead anyone. I have spent many sleepless nights trying to figure out how I was going to phase out certain players for whom I had strong feelings, but that was my job. I wasn't hired to do anything but win." – Bill Walsh

16. "Success is peace of mind, which is a direct result of self-satisfaction in knowing you did your best to become the best you are capable of becoming." – John Wooden

17. "A common mistake among those who work in sport is spending a disproportional amount of time on "x's and o's" as compared to time spent learning about people." – Mike Krzyzewski

18. "The interesting thing about coaching is that you have to trouble the comfortable, and comfort the troubled" – Ric Charlesworth

19. "All coaching is, is taking a player where he can't take himself." – Bill McCartney

20. "An acre of performance is worth a whole world of promise." – Red Auerbach

21. "Good teams become great ones when the members trust each other enough to surrender the 'me' for the 'we'" – Phil Jackson

22. "Champions keep playing until they get it right." – Billie Jean King

23. "If we were supposed to talk more than we listen we would have two mouths and one ear." – Mark Twain

24. "You can motivate by fear, and you can motivate by reward. But both those methods are only temporary. The only lasting thing is self-motivation." – Homer Rice

25. "If you have something critical to sat to a player, preface it by saying something positive. That way when you get to the criticism, at least you know he'll be listening." – Bud Grant

Conclusion

Thank you again for downloading this book!

I hope this book was able to help you to learn what it takes to be a coach, how to inspire your players, and how you can help them prepare to be the best athletes possible. You now understand how to communicate effectively. You have more ways to promote and foster teamwork and some specific tools to help your players prepare physically and mentally to become powerful winners. You also have an arsenal of winning strategies you can use to help your players adopt a winner's mindset and start building toward success.

Your next step is to find a role model to help you grow into a legendary teacher, leader, and trainer. You may choose to model yourself after a well-known professional coach, a coach in your community, or even a successful business that shares your values of high standards, hard work, admirable recruiting methods, and a willingness to continually learn and grow.

Remember, a great coach is also a great leader, so it is important to consistently present yourself as a role model to others. Always follow through on your promises, treat others the way you want to be treated, and do what you can to help others. As you model transparent trustworthiness, you lay the groundwork for others to respect you as a person; this is a solid foundation on which to build your career as a coach, a mentor, or a successful contributor in any field.

Finally, if you discovered at least one thing that has helped you or that you think would be beneficial to someone else, be sure to take a few seconds to easily post a quick positive review. As an author, your positive feedback is desperately needed. Your highly valuable five star reviews are like a river of golden joy flowing through a sunny forest of mighty trees and beautiful flowers! *To do your good deed in making the world a better place by helping others with your valuable insight, just leave a nice review.*

My Other Books and Audio Books
www.AcesEbooks.com

Popular Books

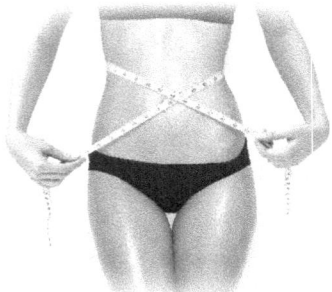

Be sure to check out my audio books as well!

 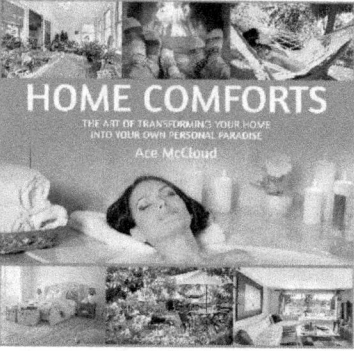 

Check out my website at: **www.AcesEbooks.com** for a complete list of all of my books and high quality audio books. I enjoy bringing you the best knowledge in the world and wish you the best in using this information to make your journey through life better and more enjoyable! **Best of luck to you!**

www.ingramcontent.com/pod-product-compliance
Lightning Source LLC
Chambersburg PA
CBHW051423070526
44584CB00023B/3555